Step by Step
Piano Course
by
Edna Mae Burnam

To Pat and Don, Peg and Pat

PLAYBACK+
Speed • Pitch • Balance • Loop

To access audio, visit:
www.halleonard.com/mylibrary

6129-9597-7200-1885

ISBN 978-1-4234-3606-5

WILLIS MUSIC

EXCLUSIVELY DISTRIBUTED BY

HAL•LEONARD®

Visit Hal Leonard Online at
www.halleonard.com

Contact us:
Hal Leonard
7777 West Bluemound Road
Milwaukee, WI 53213
Email: info@halleonard.com

In Europe, contact:
Hal Leonard Europe Limited
42 Wigmore Street
Marylebone, London, W1U 2RN
Email: info@halleonardeurope.com

In Australia, contact:
Hal Leonard Australia Pty. Ltd.
4 Lentara Court
Cheltenham, Victoria, 3192 Australia
Email: info@halleonard.com.au

FOREWORD

BOOK TWO was designed to build on the foundation established in BOOK ONE.

My aim and purpose in presenting BOOK TWO is:

- To present further rudiments of music in logical order, step by step, with gradual and steady progress.

- To provide appealing melodious pieces for the student to play and to keep these pieces within the range of his or her ability so that they may be played fluently and artistically.

- To present a challenge to the student that will increase pianistic facility.

- To provide written work in the form of musical games that will stimulate interest and further theoretical musical knowledge.

- To help strengthen the student's desire to continue to express and improve musically and to encourage an even deeper love for music.

Edna Mae Burnam

TO THE TEACHER

This is the **second** book of EDNA MAE BURNAM'S piano course STEP BY STEP.

It presents new subjects in logical order and ONE AT A TIME.

Sufficient work is given on each step so that the student will thoroughly comprehend it before going on to the next one.

In this second book, as in the first one, the subjects are covered in a clear and complete manner and "music writing games" add to the musical knowledge.

A final check-up reviews the work and ground covered. This insures **complete** understanding of previous work before going ahead to Book Three.

The student will have learned the following when this **second** book is completed:—

    1. How to name and play the following notes:—

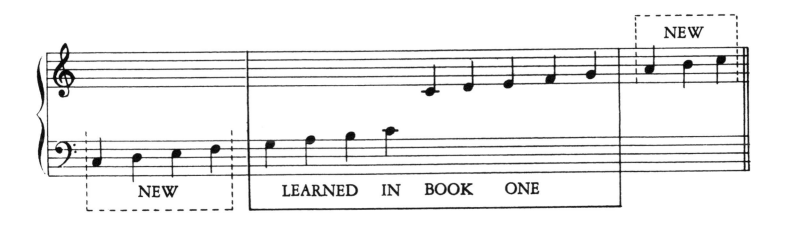

    2. Count and play eighth notes.

    3. Recognize and play sharps, flats and naturals.

    4. Play in the following key signatures:—

                 C Major — G Major — F Major.

    5. Read and play two-note chords.

    6. Cross the left hand over the right.

    7. Observe the "D.C. al fine".

MARCH OF THE PALACE GUARDS
(Review)

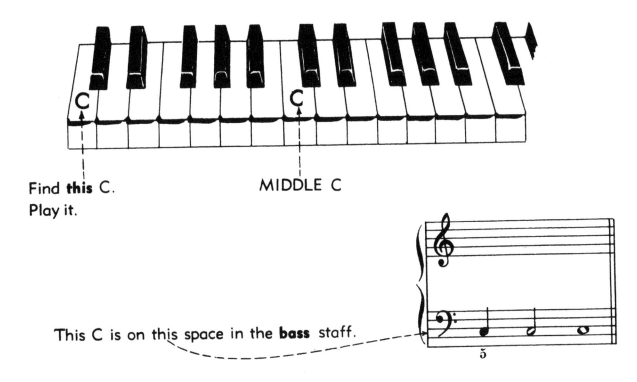

Find **this** C.
Play it.

MIDDLE C

This C is on this space in the **bass** staff.

The **left** hand plays this note even though the stem is pointing up.

Notes on the third line or below are written this way.
Play this C with the **fifth** finger of your **left** hand.

THE CLOCK

Tick, Tock, Tick, Tock, goes the clock.

Will it ev-er, ev-er stop? Ding, Dong, Ding. Ding, Dong, Ding.

8

SUBMARINES

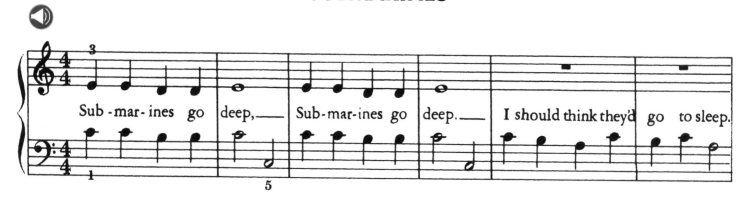

Sub-mar-ines go | deep,____ | Sub-mar-ines go | deep.____ | I should think they'd | go to sleep.

I should think they'd | go to sleep. | In the sea so | deep.____ | In the sea so | deep.

STILL ANOTHER C

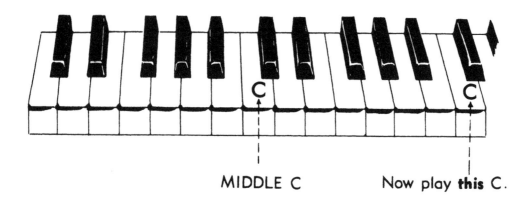

MIDDLE C   Now play **this** C.

Here are some pictures of this C.

This C is on this space in the **treble** staff.

The **right** hand plays this note even though the stem is pointing down.

Notes on the third line or above are written this way.

Play this C with the **fifth** finger of your **right** hand.

SLEEPY HEAD

TELEPHONE POLES

Tel - e - phone poles, reach - ing way up high. Tel - e - phone poles say "hel - lo" to the sky.

TWO BIG BLACKBIRDS

Two big black - birds on a hill.

One named Jack and one named Jill. Off goes Jack, Off goes Jill. Come back Jack! Come back Jill!

MAILBOXES

Here are pictures of mailboxes.

See the notes in each mailbox?

Write the name of each note directly under it.

If you get them all right, the mailman will know where to deliver your mail.

KITES

Look at these kites.

To fly well, they must be balanced just right.

To **play** well, we must know **note values** well.

Put as many bows on the tail of each kite as there are **counts** to the **notes** in each kite.

A note like this ♩ gets one count.

So you will know how to do this game, one is finished for you.

FROGS

Each frog croaks **four** measures.

They are croaking in either $\frac{2}{4}$ $\frac{3}{4}$ or $\frac{4}{4}$ time.

Write the correct **time signatures** before each line.

Write the **counts** under the **notes** and **rests**—like this

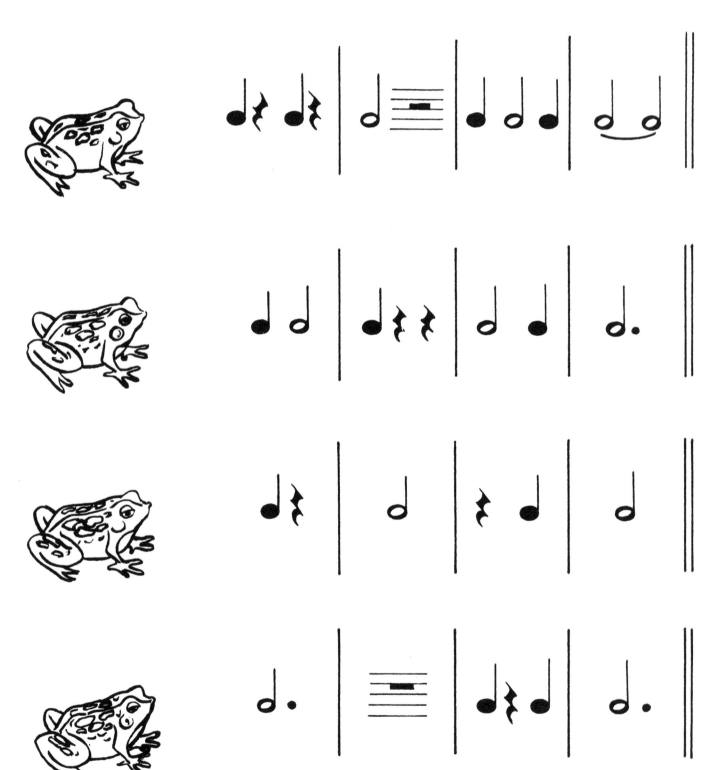

TV

F ON KEYBOARD

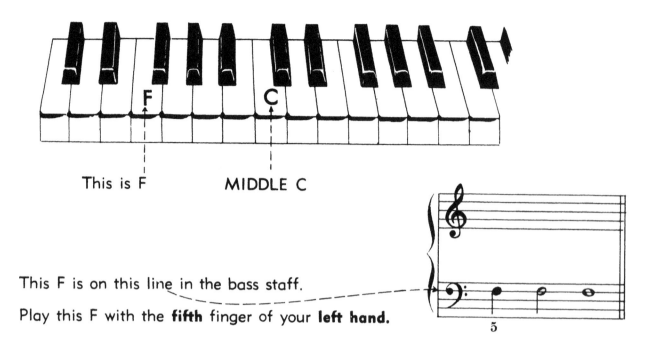

This is F   MIDDLE C

This F is on this line in the bass staff.

Play this F with the **fifth** finger of your **left hand.**

WHEN I TAKE A TRIP

When I take a trip I al-ways like to come back home.

WALTZ

THE FLAT SIGN

This is a **flat** sign ♭

When a flat is placed **before** a note, play the **nearest** key to the **left of the note.**

This is B flat
Play B flat

MIDDLE C

If this same B is repeated in the **same measure,** you must **still play B flat!**
After a bar line the note must have another flat sign **before** it if it is to be played as B flat.

B flat

B—**not** B flat

HALLOWEEN

Hal - lo - ween is | com - ing,

It is ver - y | near. | Hal - lo - ween is | com - ing, It is al - most | here.

THE NATURAL SIGN

This is a natural sign ♮

When a **natural** sign is placed **before** a note it **cancels** the flat.

FUZZY LITTLE CATERPILLAR

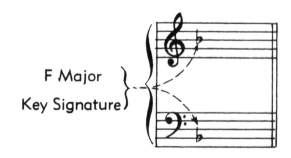

THE FLAT SIGN IN THE KEY SIGNATURE—F Major

When a flat sign is placed next to the **clef signs** (to the right), it becomes the **key signature.**

One flat is the **key of F major.** This flat is B.

When you see one flat in the **key signature,** you must remember to flat every B.

F Major
Key Signature

JOLLY LITTLE PENGUINS

MY VENETIAN BLINDS

My Ven - e - tian blinds are play-ing peek-a - boo.

I will pull the cord and let the sun-shine through.

EVERY LITTLE LAWNMOWER

Eve - ry lit - tle lawn-mower on the street,

Gives the grass a hair - cut, Keeps it ver - y neat.

EIGHTH NOTES

Here is an **eighth** note (a **running** note) ♪ Notice the little flag on the stem.

An eighth note gets **one-half a count.**

It takes **two** eighth notes to get **one** count.

Sometimes when there are two eighth notes together, instead of making them like this ♪ ♪

the flags are joined together, and they look like this ♫

When they are **joined** together like this ♫ the **two notes get one count** ♫

One

Here is a piece that has eighth notes in $\frac{2}{4}$ time.

Count it—and **clap** as you count. Then **play** it and **count** it.

Play it **s l o w l y** so that you will be able to keep good time when you reach the eighth notes.

A.

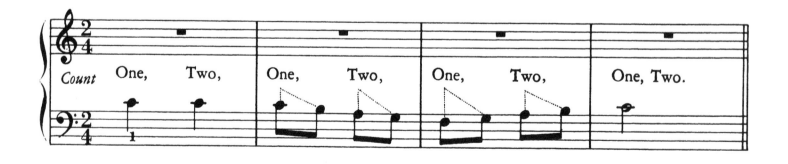

Eighth notes may also be joined together like this

Count them—and **clap** as you count. Then **play** and **count** them.

Here is some music in $\frac{4}{4}$ time for you to count and play.

Play it **s l o w l y .**

B.

Here is music in $\frac{3}{4}$ time.

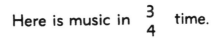

C.

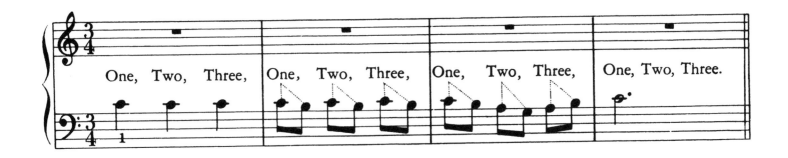

JOLLY LITTLE ROLLER COASTER

THE SHARP SIGN

This is a **sharp** sign ♯

When a sharp is placed **before a note,** play the **nearest** key to the **right of the note.**

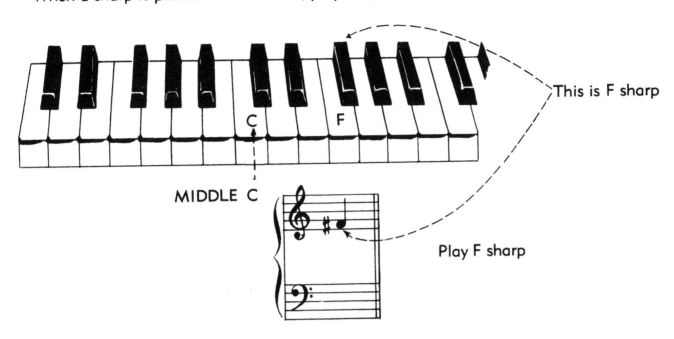

MIDDLE C

This is F sharp

Play F sharp

If this same F is repeated **in the same measure,** you must still play F sharp! **After** a bar line the note must have **another** sharp sign **before** it if it is to be played as F sharp.

F sharp

F—**not** F sharp

SLEEPY HEAD

When I wake up eve-ry—day, I'm a sleep-y head.

When I wake up eve-ry—day, I want to stay in bed.

AUTUMN LEAVES

Au-tumn leaves are fall-ing, fall-ing, fall-ing.

Au-tumn leaves are fall - ing on the ground.

When a natural sign ♮ is placed **before** a note, it **cancels** the sharp.

BABIES

Ba - bies can't do ver - y much. They can't e - ven walk!

Ba - bies can't do ver - y much. They can't e - ven talk!

JINGLE BELLS

Words and Music by J. Pierpont
arr. E.M.B.

Jin - gle bells, Jin - gle bells, Jin - gle all the way.

Oh, what fun it is to ride in a one-horse o - pen sleigh!

Jin - gle bells, Jin - gle bells, Jin - gle all the way.

Oh, what fun it is to ride in a one-horse o - pen sleigh!

THE SHARP SIGN IN THE KEY SIGNATURE—G Major

When a sharp sign is placed next to the **clef signs,** (to the right), it becomes the **key signature.**

One sharp is the key of G major. This sharp is F.

When you see one sharp in the **key signature,** you must remember to **sharp every F.**

G major
Key signature

LITTLE CHIPMUNK

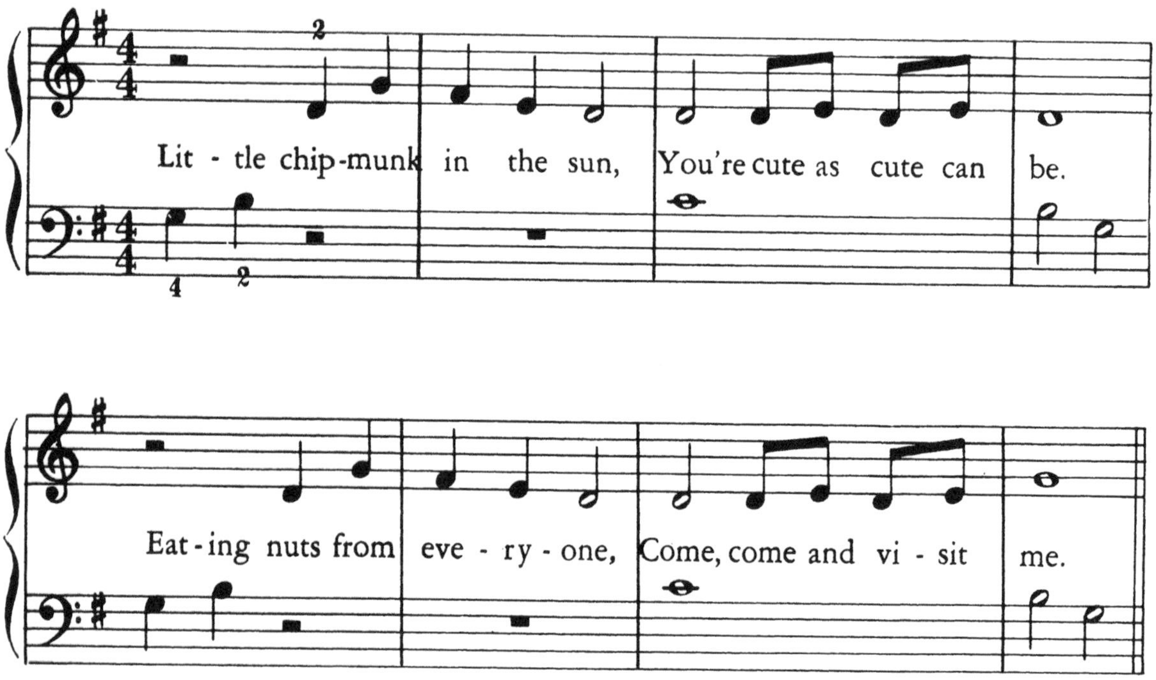
Lit - tle chip-munk in the sun, You're cute as cute can be.
Eat-ing nuts from eve - ry - one, Come, come and vi - sit me.

ICE SKATING

THREE BLIND MICE

Traditional

Three blind mice.

Three blind mice.

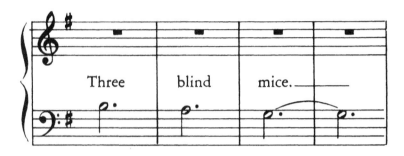

See how they run, See how they run, They all run af-ter the

farm-er's wife, She cut off their tails with a carv-ing knife. Did you

ev-er see such a sight in your life, As three blind mice?

ELEPHANTS

Here are some elephants.

How many logs can each one carry?

This is the way to find out.

Each one can carry as many logs as there are **counts** in the **notes** on his blanket.

A note like this ♩ gets one count.

Write how many logs each one can carry in the space under each elephant.

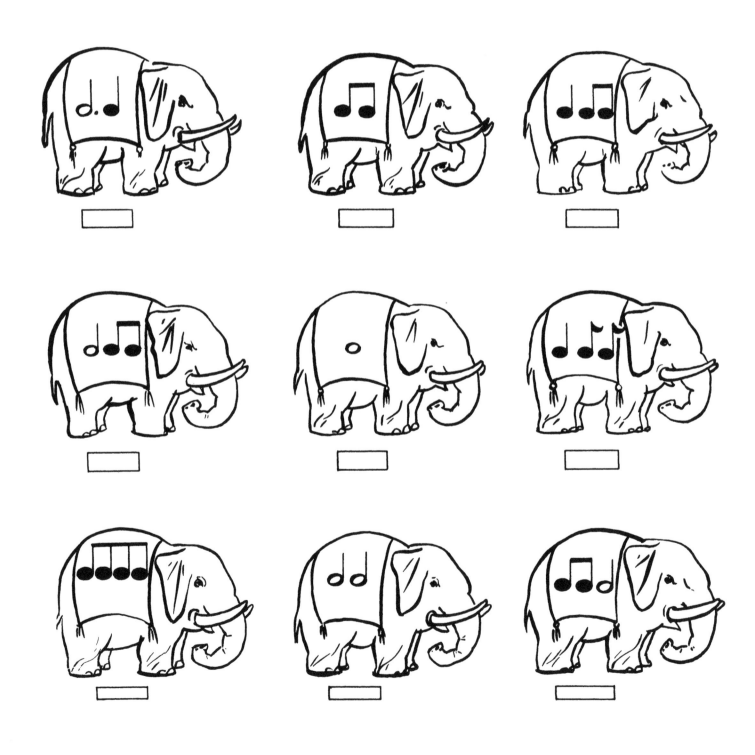

HENS

Here are some hens.

Each hen clucks four measures.

They cluck in either $\frac{2}{4}$, $\frac{3}{4}$ or $\frac{4}{4}$ time.

Write the correct time signature before each line.

Then write the counts under the notes—like this:

TWO-NOTE CHORDS

When **two** or **more notes** are played **together,** they are called a **chord.**

Here is a two-note chord

Here are some pieces with two-note chords.

TUNE OF THE TUBA

I GO TO SCHOOL

I go to school eve-ry morn - ing, with my friend.____

FLAT, SHARP, AND NATURAL SIGNS

REMEMBER:—

When a flat sign ♭ is placed before a note, play the **nearest** key to the **left** of the note.

When a sharp sign ♯ is placed before a note, play the **nearest** key to the **right** of the note.

When a natural sign ♮ is placed before a note, it **cancels** the effect of a sharp or flat sign.

JAPANESE FAN

A NEW E

This new note is E.

This E is on this ---- space of the bass staff.

Play this C with the **fifth** finger of your left hand.

Play this C and then play the E above it.

Play this E with your **third** finger.

Now play this.

CLIMBING A MONKEY BAR

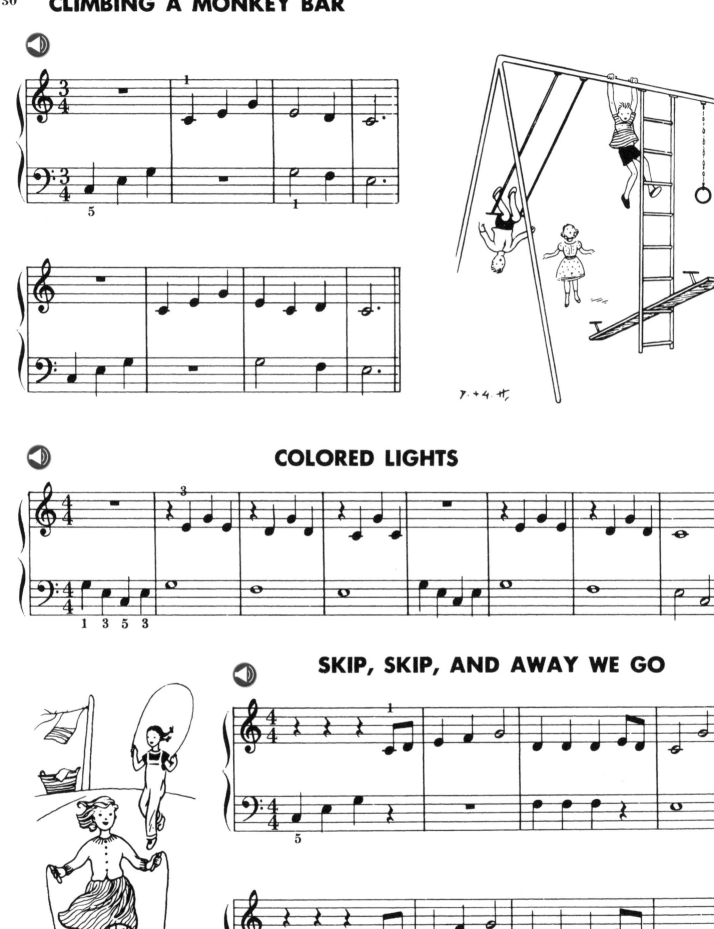

COLORED LIGHTS

SKIP, SKIP, AND AWAY WE GO

A NEW D

5

Play this C with the **fifth finger** of your **left** hand.

This D is on this line of the bass staff.

Now play the **next white note above** it.

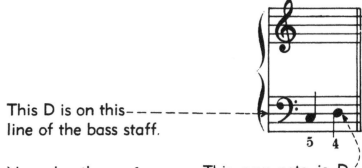

5 4

This new note is D. Play this D with the **fourth** finger of your left hand.

SONG OF THE CELLO

RAINBOW

When I   see a   rain-bow in the sky,

Beau-ti-ful and bright.__ When I   see a   rain-bow in the sky,   It's   a   pret-ty   sight.__

EARLY IN THE MORNING

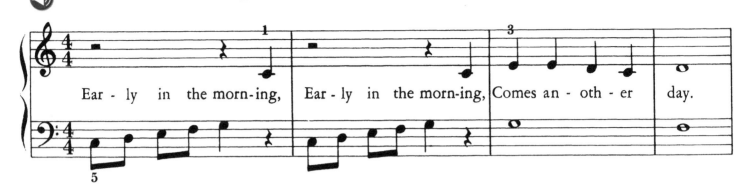

Ear - ly in the morn-ing, Ear - ly in the morn-ing, Comes an - oth - er day.

Ear - ly in the morn-ing, Ear - ly in the morn-ing, Night has gone a - way.

ARE YOU SLEEPING

Traditional

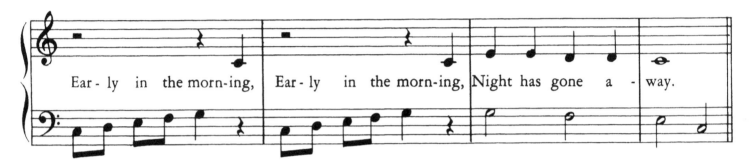

Are you sleep-ing? Are you sleep-ing?

Broth - er John, Broth - er John.

Morn-ing bells are ring - ing, Morn-ing bells are ring - ing! Ding, Dong, Ding! Ding, Dong, Ding!

NEW NOTE   A   (on treble staff)

This is A—**above** MIDDLE C

This A is on this **space** of the **treble** staff

The piece SWINGING has this A in it.

Can you find these A's?

Notice that the letters (l.h.) are in three places in this piece.

These letters (l.h.) mean that your **left** hand must play this note.

To do this, your **left hand must cross over your right hand.**

The dotted lines in the first two measures are a guide to help you cross your **left** hand **over** your **right** to play this A.

SWINGING

I can swing up high. Near - ly to the sky.

I can near - ly touch the sky or I can try!

CHANGE OF FINGERING

Finger marks are a **great** help to you when you play the piano.

Always use the fingers that are **marked** for you when you play.

Your playing will sound **smooth,** and it will be **easier** for you.

Notice that you begin playing the next piece by using your third finger on F.

If you **begin** this way, you will be able to play A with your **right** hand, using your fifth finger.

EVERY SUNDAY MORNING

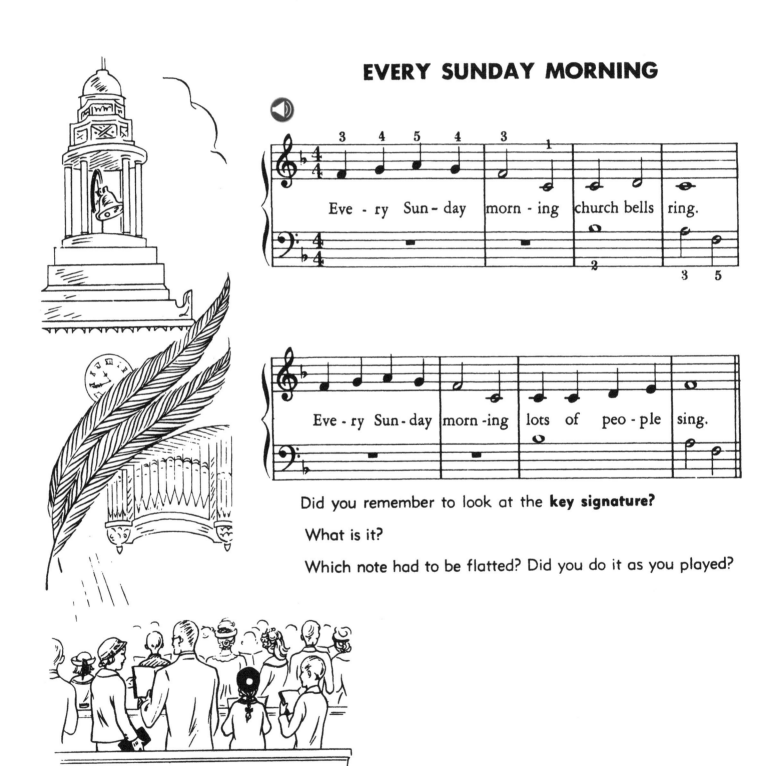

Eve - ry Sun - day morn - ing church bells ring.

Eve - ry Sun - day morn - ing lots of peo - ple sing.

Did you remember to look at the **key signature?**

What is it?

Which note had to be flatted? Did you do it as you played?

D.C. al Fine

Look at the last measure of this piece.

Notice what is printed over it— **D.C. al fine.**

When you see this in a piece, it means that you must go back to the beginning of the piece again —and play it until you come to the word **"fine".**

You will find the word "Fine" in the eighth measure of this piece.

"Fine" means that the piece **ends** there.

FUNNY LITTLE BUNNY

Fun - ny lit - tle bun - ny with your ears so long.

Fine

Fun - ny lit - tle bun - ny, can you sing this song?

Hop - ping, Hop - ping, Nev - er stop - ping, Hop - ping, here and there. l.h. (over)

D.C. al fine

Hop - ping, Hop - ping, Nev - er stop - ping, Hop - ping, eve - ry - where. l.h. (over)

Did you remember to **cross** your **left** hand in the last measure of the **third** and **fourth** lines?

ROCKING CHAIR

When I rock in my old rock-ing chair,

Fine

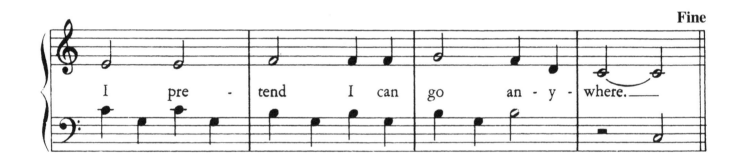

I pre-tend I can go an-y-where._____

Mm_____ mm_____ mm_____ mm_____

D.C. al fine

mm_____ mm_____ mm_____ mm.

CHRISTMAS STOCKINGS

Here are some Christmas Stockings.

How many presents will there be in each stocking on Christmas morning?

This is how to find out.

There will be as many presents as there are **counts** in the **notes** on each stocking.

Write the number of counts on the top of each stocking.

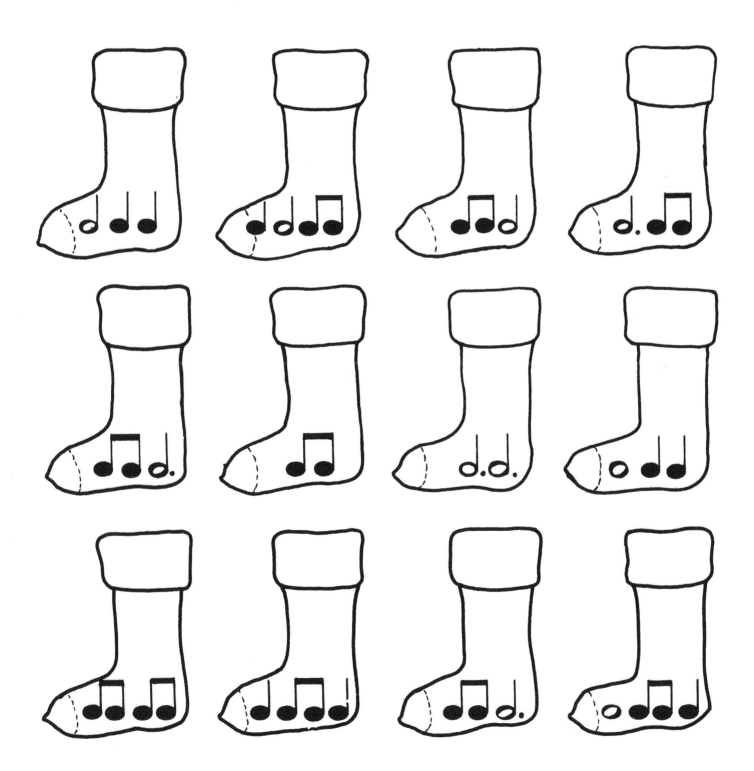

BIRDS

Each of these birds sings four measures.

They sing in either $\frac{2}{4}$, $\frac{3}{4}$ or $\frac{4}{4}$ time.

Write the correct time signature before each line.

Then write the counts under each note.

A BALLOON

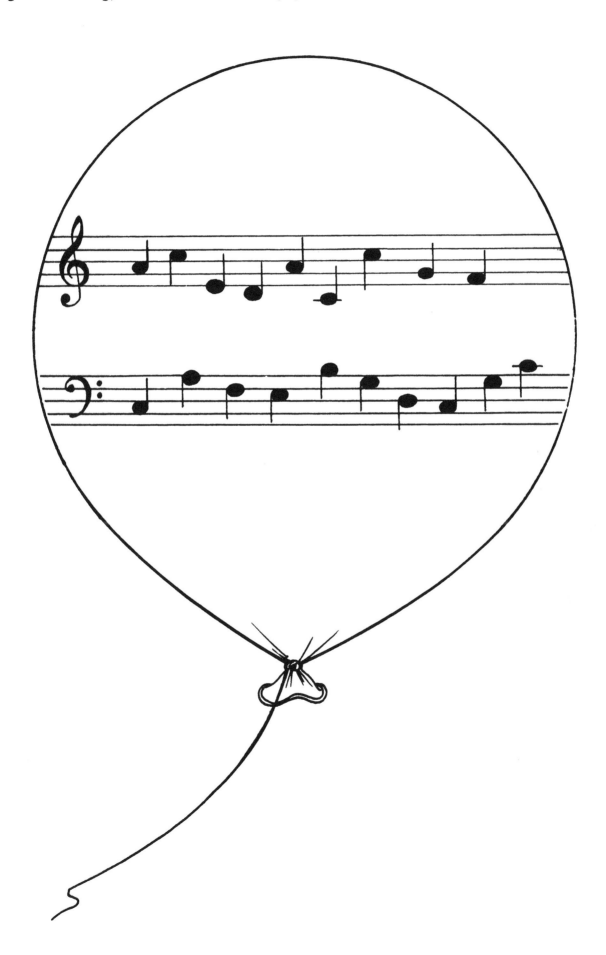

Write the name of each note under the note.
If you get one wrong, it means the balloon pops!

40

JACK-O-LANTERNS

Here are some Halloween Jack-O-Lanterns.

Write the names of the notes below each Jack-O-Lantern.

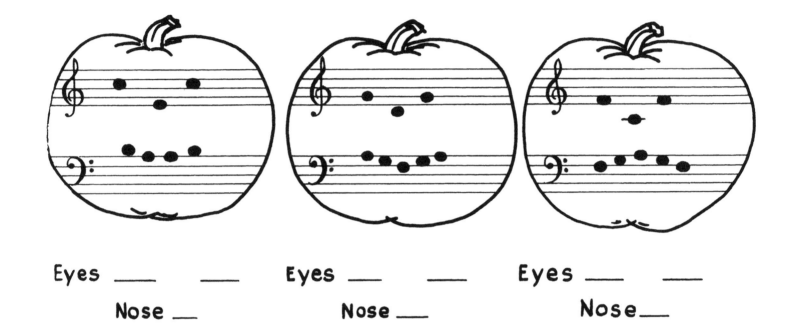

Eyes ___ ___

Nose ___

Mouth ___ ___ ___

Eyes ___ ___

Nose ___

Mouth ___ ___ ___ ___

Eyes ___ ___

Nose ___

Mouth ___ ___ ___ ___

Eyes ___ ___ ___

Nose ___

Mouth ___ ___ ___

Eyes ___ ___

Nose ___

Mouth ___ ___ ___

Eyes ___ ___ ___

Nose ___

Mouth ___ ___ ___

A NEW B (on treble staff)

This is B **above** MIDDLE C

This B is on this line of the treble staff

When you play the pieces below,
make sure you use the correct fingers.

LITTLE MOUSE

Nib - ble, Nib - ble, Nib - ble, Goes a lit - tle mouse.

Nib - ble, Nib - ble, Nib - ble, All a - round the house.

CLOWNS

42

PRAIRIE SONG

When I ride on the plains far a-way, I sing a far-a-way song.____

Fine

When I ride on the plains far a-way, I sing it all the day long.____

List-en to the song of the prai-rie,____ List-en to a song far a-way.____

D.C. al fine

List-en to the song of the prai-rie,____ Hear the song to-day.____

FINAL CHECK-UP

Your teacher will give you this final check-up.

Show me a note that gets :—

   1 count
   2 counts
   3 counts
   4 counts
   ½ a count

Show me **two** notes that get **one** count.

Show me a rest that gets :—

   1 count
   2 counts
   4 counts
   3 counts

Show me a :—

   sharp
   flat
   natural
   two note chord

Show me the following key signatures :—

   F major
   C major
   G major

Explain what "D.C. al fine" means.

Explain what "l.h." means.

Certificate of Merit

This certifies that

....

has successfully completed

BOOK TWO
OF
EDNA MAE BURNAM'S
PIANO COURSE

STEP BY STEP

and is eligible for promotion to

BOOK THREE

.... Teacher

Date..

Edna Mae Burnam was a pioneer in piano publishing. The creator of the iconic *A Dozen a Day* technique series and *Step by Step* method was born on September 15, 1907 in Sacramento, California. She began lessons with her mother, a piano teacher who drove a horse and buggy daily through the Sutter Buttes mountain range to reach her students. In college Burnam decided that she too enjoyed teaching young children, and majored in elementary education at California State University (then Chico State College) with a minor in music. She spent several years teaching kindergarten in public schools before starting her own piano studio and raising daughters Pat and Peggy. She delighted in composing for her students, and took theory and harmony lessons from her husband David (a music professor and conductor of the Sacramento Symphony in the 1940s).

Burnam began submitting original pieces to publishers in the mid-1930s, and was thrilled when one of them, "The Clock That Stopped," was accepted, even though her remuneration was a mere $20. Undaunted, the industrious composer sent in the first *A Dozen a Day* manuscript to her Willis editor in 1950, complete with stick-figure sketches for each exercise. Her editor loved the simple genius of the playful artwork resembling a musical technique, and so did students and teachers: the book rapidly blossomed into a series of seven and continues to sell millions of copies. In 1959, the first book in the *Step by Step* series was published, with hundreds of individual songs and pieces along the way, often identified by whimsical titles in Burnam's trademark style.

The immense popularity of her books solidified Edna Mae Burnam's place and reputation in music publishing history, yet throughout her lifetime she remained humble and effervescent. "I always left our conversations feeling upbeat and happy," says Kevin Cranley, Willis president. "She could charm the legs off a piano bench," Bob Sylva of the *Sacramento Bee* wrote, "make a melody out of a soap bubble, and a song out of a moon beam."

Burnam died in 2007, a few months shy of her 100th birthday. "Music enriches anybody's life, even if you don't turn out to be musical," she said once in an interview. "I can't imagine being in a house without a piano."

STEP INTO SUCCESS...
with Step by Step!

By Edna Mae Burnam

  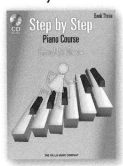 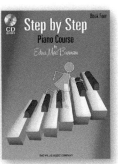 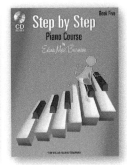 

The *Step by Step Piano Course* provides students with an opportunity to learn the piano in a unique and charming way, with each lesson presented in a logical order and at a manageable pace.

METHOD BOOKS

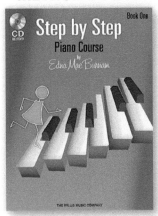

Book 1	00416766 (Book/CD)....	$9.95
	00414712 (Book only)...	$6.99
Book 2	00416767 (Book/CD)....	$9.95
	00414713 (Book only)...	$6.99
Book 3	00416768 (Book/CD)..	$10.95
	00414716 (Book only)..	$7.99
Book 4	00416769 (Book/Audio)	$10.99
	00414845 (Book only)..	$7.99
Book 5	00416770 (Book/Audio)	$11.99
	00414846 (Book only)..	$7.99
Book 6	00416771 (Book/CD)..	$11.99
	00414847 (Book only)..	$7.99

SOLO BOOKS

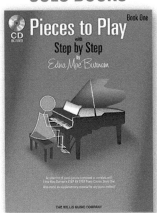

Book 1	00416772 (Book/CD)...	$9.95
	00404507 (Book only)..	$5.99
Book 2	00416773 (Book/CD)...	$9.95
	00404508 (Book only)..	$5.99
Book 3	00416774 (Book/CD)...	$9.95
	00404550 (Book only)..	$5.99
Book 4	00416775 (Book/CD)...	$9.95
	00404567 (Book only)..	$5.99
Book 5	00416776 (Book/CD)...	$9.99
	00404604 (Book only)..	$5.99
Book 6	00416777 (Book/CD)...	$9.99
	00404627 (Book only)..	$5.99

THEORY BOOKS

Book 1	00404471 (Book only)..	$5.99
Book 2	00404472 (Book only)..	$5.99
Book 3	00404473 (Book only)..	$5.99
Book 4	00404476 (Book only)..	$5.99
Book 5	00404477 (Book only)..	$5.99
Book 6	00404478 (Book only)...	$5.99

ALSO AVAILABLE: ALL-IN-ONE

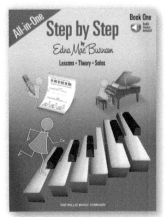

Book 1 00158461 (Book/Audio) .$14.99

CHRISTMAS

Book 1 00278591 (Book/Audio) ..$9.99

www.willispianomusic.com

WILLIS MUSIC

EXCLUSIVELY DISTRIBUTED BY

HAL•LEONARD®

0618

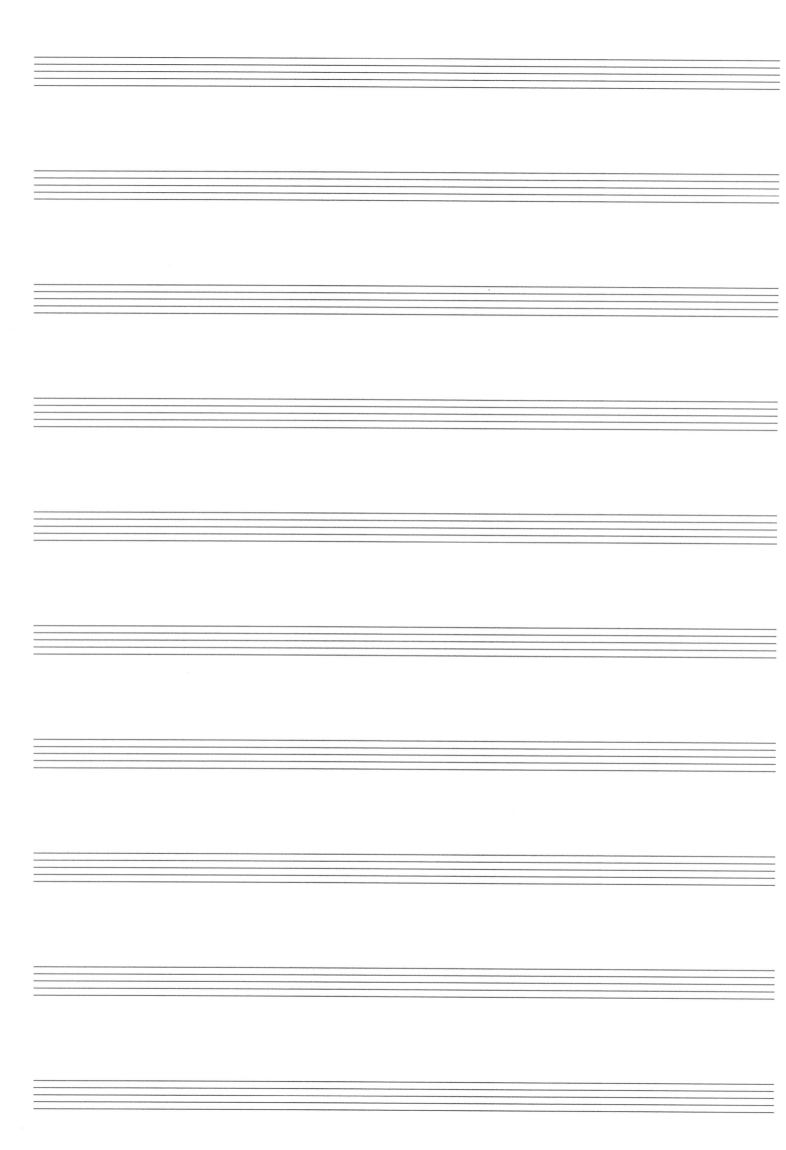